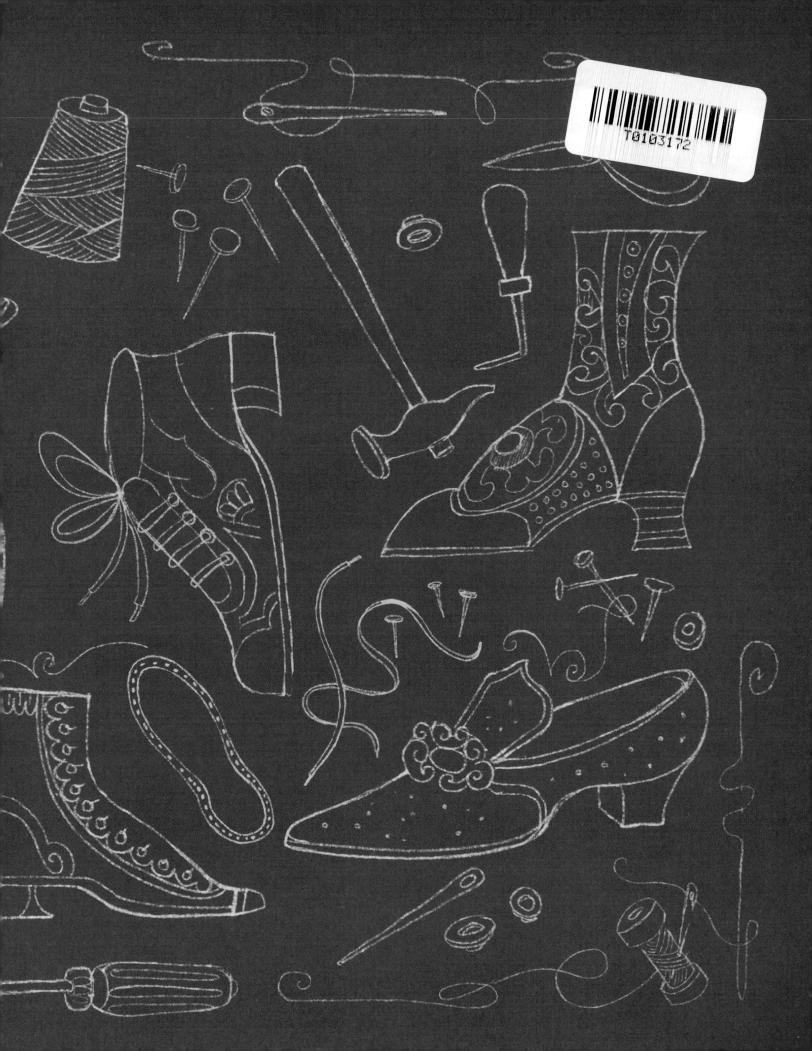

For my Uncle Steve,
the original King of STEM
—Shana

For Miles and Jennie
—Stephen

Sleeping Bear Press™

2395 South Huron Parkway, Suite 200, Ann Arbor, MI 48104
www.sleepingbearpress.com © Sleeping Bear Press
Printed and bound in South Korea
10 9 8 7 6 5 4 3 2 1

Library of Congress Cataloging-in-Publication Data
Names: Keller, Shana, 1977- author. | Costanza, Stephen, illustrator.
Title: The sole man / [by] Shana Keller ; [illustrated by] Stephen Costanza.
Description: Ann Arbor, MI : Sleeping Bear Press, [2024] | Audience: Ages 6-10 | Summary: "In 1873, Jan Ernst Matzeliger arrived
in America. He was highly skilled with machinery, but no one wanted to hire a Black immigrant. Jan finally got a job at a shoe factory.
He envisioned a machine that would help shoe production, but people scoffed at him. Despite obstacles, he persevered"-- Provided by publisher.
Identifiers: LCCN 2024005269 | ISBN 9781534113008 (hardcover) | Subjects: LCSH: Matzeliger, Jan Ernst, 1852-1889. | Shoemakers--United
States--Biography--Juvenile literature. | Shoe industry--United States--Biography--Juvenile literature. | Inventors, Black--United
States--Biography--Juvenile literature. | Immigrants--Employment--United
States--Juvenile literature. | LCGFT: Biographies Classification: LCC
HD9787.U62 M3754 2024 | DDC 338.4768531092
[B]--dc23/eng/20240312 | LC record available at
https://lccn.loc.gov/2024005269

THE
SOLE MAN

WRITTEN BY SHANA KELLER AND
ILLUSTRATED BY STEPHEN COSTANZA

Jan took a deep breath. He held the diagrams and instructions in his hands, instructions so complex that the United States Patent Office had sent an inspector to investigate. They didn't think the machine Jan invented could be real.

A patent would protect Jan's rights as the sole inventor of his machine. If the patent was approved, Jan would be able to license his invention and make money off of it.

"Sir, I present to you, my lasting machine," Jan said. His voice was strong, but his hands shook a little as the inspector slowly stepped around the giant machine, eyeing it this way and that.

This wasn't the first model Jan had built; it wasn't even his first machine. Jan had grown up in Suriname, in South America, around machines that whirred, purred, clunked, and clanked.

As a young boy, he worked in his father's mechanic shops building, fixing, and tinkering.

Jan had to stop himself from tinkering now while the inspector poked at his machine.

"This was all your idea?" the inspector asked.

Jan nodded and told the inspector about his first job in America.

When he was nineteen, Jan had left South America and
his father's workshops on a merchant ship. He ventured
across the ocean from one continent to another.

Two years later Jan landed in Philadelphia, Pennsylvania, the "Workshop of the World." The city clamored and clanged with hundreds of factories . . . and jobs.

If only he spoke English! Jan spoke Dutch, which made it hard to communicate. He didn't have the right skin color, either.

Although the American Civil War had ended nearly a decade earlier, no one wanted to hire a Black immigrant who couldn't speak English.

But Jan didn't give up. He tried and tried until, finally, he found a job in one of Philadelphia's factories—a shoe factory!

Jan was relieved. The machines he saw and learned how to use spoke in a language he was familiar with.

It was there that Jan first used the McKay—named after its inventor, Gordon McKay—to produce shoes.

A. SMITH
SHOES
No. 348

The McKay stitched two pieces of leather together to make the bottom part of the shoe, called the sole. Then a skilled worker, a hand laster, wrapped a smooth piece of leather around a wooden foot model called a *last*.

To hold the upper shoe's material in place, the hand laster punched holes into the leather using nails. Then he sewed that piece to the sole by hand.

The job required twelve to sixteen stitches per inch.

A good hand laster could only make twenty to thirty pairs of shoes per week. This slowed down the manufacturing process and made shoes a luxury.

Jan wondered why there weren't any machines
to connect the upper piece of a shoe to the sole.

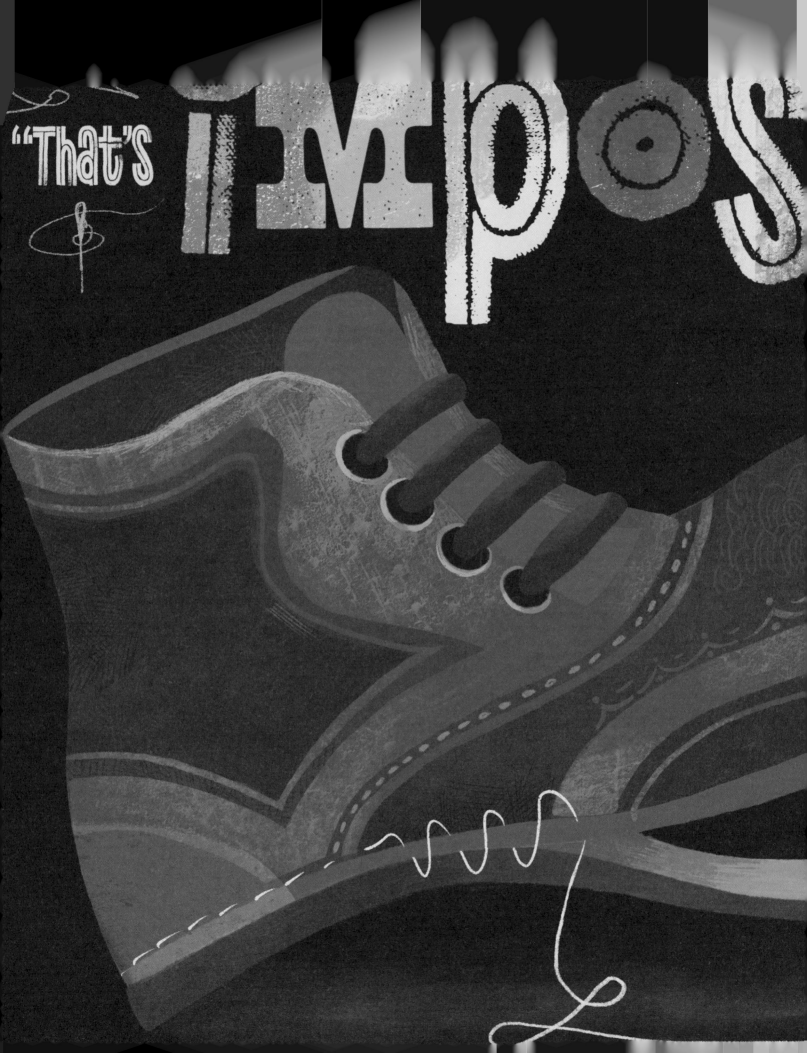

SiBLe!"

One hand laster laughed. "You have to sew the top part first. Then *shape* it over the last, line the material up perfectly—which is hard to do—hold it steady, punch the holes, and then sew them together."

Jan remembered studying each step for so long, the hand laster scoffed at him.

"If the shoe manufacturers can't mechanize this process, what makes you think you can?" he asked. "No one can create such a thing!"

Perhaps, but Jan had grown up
using tools and fixing machines. Ideas looped
in his mind like thread through a needle. Jan didn't have a lot
of money, but he saved what he could, and a couple of
years later he moved to Lynn, Massachusetts,
the "Shoe Capital of the World."

Once again, it took him a while to find a job, but he was eventually hired at the Harney Brothers' shoe factory. There Jan used new machines that produced different parts of the shoe.

One machine cut out the upper parts of the shoe, and another one created the holes for the buttons.

But . . .

Just like in Philadelphia, Jan saw the same problem.
He asked the same questions. And got the same answers.

No one thought he could invent a
machine that would mold the upper
part of the shoe to a last, then
sew it to the sole.

HARNEY BROS.

He was discouraged when people didn't support him or believe in his idea.

But Jan stayed focused, and he believed in himself.

Now, after three long years of planning, drawing, and testing, Jan's eyes shone and his heart raced. It was time to share his invention.

The machine stood taller than Jan and took up most of the space in the small room he rented.

"How does it work?" the inspector asked.

Jan remembered the cold months and long nights it had taken to make his first model, a prototype. The prototype was made from cheap materials like cigar boxes, wire, and scrap metal. The materials weren't strong, but they were all he could afford.

To make the prototype, Jan drew diagrams of what he thought each step in the shoemaking process would require. He used other machines in the shoemaking process as a reference point. He also went to night school to improve his English and art skills.

When his drawings were finished, he labeled every part. Then he sketched out the individual pieces that would make up the machine.

VOLUME

Fig.10

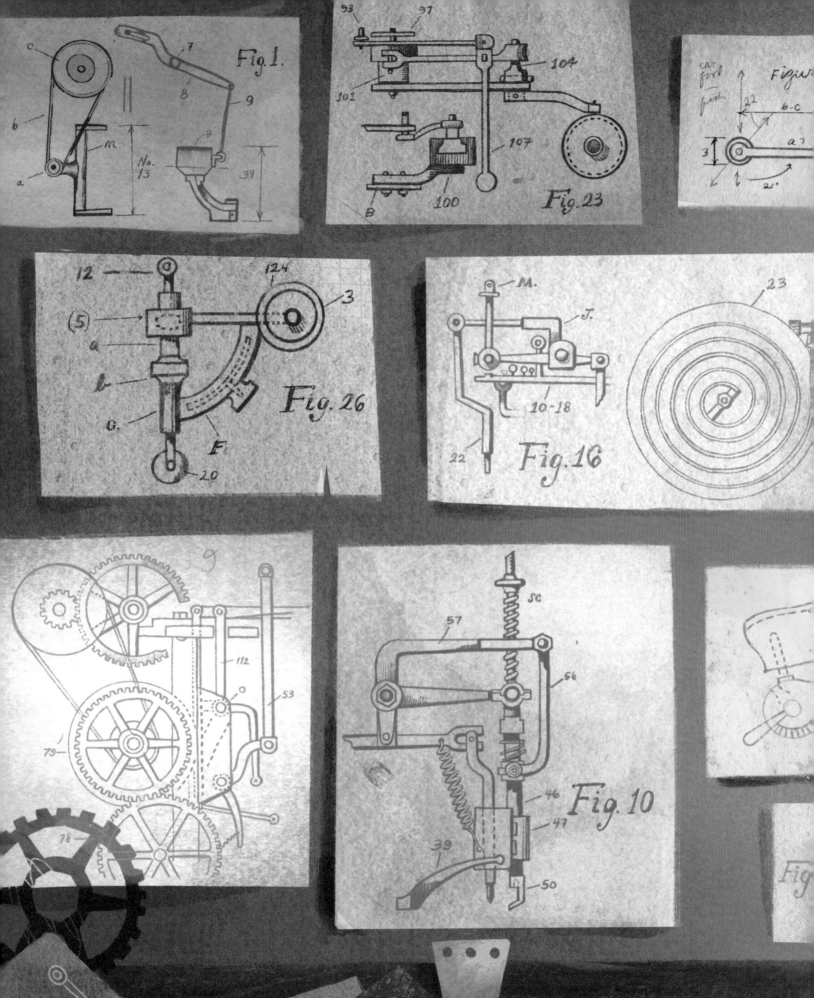

Following these detailed drawings, Jan built the parts, then used those parts to assemble his model.

"Allow me to demonstrate," Jan said.

Jan put the materials in place. He set the dials and pulled the levers.

The machine did exactly what the hand laster said it couldn't do.

It stretched and molded the upper leather to the foot last. It lined the material up perfectly with the sole. It held the shaped leather piece down, punched the holes, and lastly, sewed the pieces together.

"My goodness!" The inspector circled the
giant contraption in the small room. He watched
in awe as Jan's lasting machine spit out
one completed shoe after another.

Jan had tinkered and tinkered until his
lasting machine could make up to
seven hundred shoes in one day!

His patent was approved.

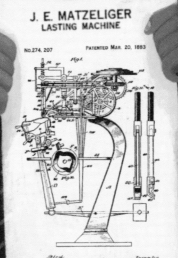

7 Sheets—Sheet 7.

ELIGER.
CHINE.
Patented Mar. 20, 1893

Inventor

Jan E. Matzeliger

Fig. 26.

Fig. 29.

Jan E. Matzeliger
Inventor

Jan Earnst (also spelled Ernst) Matzeliger was born in 1852 to a Suriname mother of African descent and a Dutch father of Anglo descent. He was raised in Paramaribo, Suriname, South America. Records indicate that Jan's mother was enslaved and that he was cared for by his paternal aunt.

Growing up, Jan worked in multiple shops run by his father. By the time he was ten years old, Jan could repair machines and use a lathe. When Jan was nineteen, he joined the crew of an East Indian merchant ship. In 1873, after two years of seafaring, Jan immigrated to America.

Although slavery had ended in America nearly a decade before, no one wanted to hire the young man of color who couldn't speak English. Jan initially had no formal education; however, he was a master of tools and machines. He eventually found a job at a shoe factory in Philadelphia, Pennsylvania.

When he moved to Lynn, Massachusetts, Jan attended formal school. He took night classes to improve his English and study science. He was also an avid oil painter.

Jan faced multiple discriminatory challenges. As an immigrant of color, his pay was unethically low compared to the pay of other employees with similar skills. Jan worked on the weekends as a coach driver and often skipped meals in order to save money.

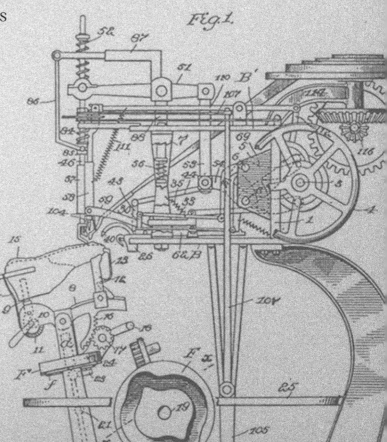

Once his model was complete, Jan created the Union Lasting Machine Company with two people willing to invest in him. Together, they helped fund the materials and supplies he needed to make the prototype.

When the United States government granted Jan a patent for his invention in 1883, the lasting machine was not initially welcomed. Factory workers ridiculed his idea. Perhaps they feared they would be replaced by the machine. But the truth was, Jan's invention created thousands more jobs. Many shoe companies saw its potential and wanted to use Jan's invention.

Unfortunately, Jan didn't get to enjoy his success for long. Late nights at school, working extra jobs, and skipping out on meals to save money contributed to Jan's poor health. He contracted tuberculosis and died in 1889, six years after he received his patent. Though his life was short, Jan's remarkable invention left an enduring impact on the world. Jan's machine lasted and *lasted* all around the world. His design spurred a billion-dollar industry that increased shoe production by nearly 1,000 percent and is still used today.

In 1991, to honor Jan E. Matzeliger, the United States Postal Service issued a commemorative stamp designed by Barbara Higgins Bond. The 29¢ stamp is part of the Black Heritage stamp series and features Jan and his design of the shoe lasting machine.